"I'll Pray Anyway"

THE STORY OF DANIEL

By Marilyn Lashbrook

Illustrated by Stephanie McFetridge Britt

Presented to...

__Bryn_____

From

Thurso Baptist church

26th June 2016

**CANDLE
BOOKS**

Daniel in the Lions' Den is a favourite with children. And this book will make the story even more fun for your preschool child. The story of Daniel will help your child learn the importance of prayer. This would be a good time to teach your child to pray simple sentence prayers, like "Thank you, God, for this sunny day," "Help me, God, to obey." "I love you, God, and I'm glad you love me."

Copyright © Rainbow Studies International

First published in the UK in 1994 by Candle Books (a publishing imprint of Lion Hudson plc). This printing 2004

Distributed by Marston Book Services Ltd, PO Box 269, Abingdon, Oxon OX14 4YN

Co-edition arranged by Lion Hudson plc, Oxford

All enquiries to Lion Hudson plc, Mayfield House, 256 Banbury Road, Oxford, OX2 7DH

Tel: +44 (0) 1865 302750
Fax: +44 (0) 1865 302757
Email: coed@lionhudson.com
www.lionhudson.com

Printed in Hong Hong

ISBN 0 9489 0295 7

"I'LL PRAY ANYWAY"

THE STORY OF DANIEL

By Marilyn Lashbrook

Illustrated by Stephanie McFetridge Britt

Taken from Daniel 6

The sun
was just waking up
when Daniel
leaped out of bed.

Why was Daniel up so early?
He wanted to pray.
He prayed every day.

Daniel was one of the king's best workers.
He needed God's help
to do a good job.

The king praised Daniel
for his good work.
This made the other workers ANGRY!

So they decided to trick the king
into signing a rule
that would get Daniel into trouble.

The king made a big mistake
and signed their silly rule.
It said anyone who prayed to God

would be thrown into
a den of LIONS! . . .
HUNGRY LIONS . . .
with ENORMOUS TEETH!

Daniel heard about the rule.
"I'll pray anyway," he thought.

"Nobody, not even the king
has the right
to make a rule like that!"

Daniel went straight to his home
. . . and prayed.

He knew God would hear.
He knew God would help.

The men who hated Daniel
saw him praying.
They could not wait
to get him in trouble.

So they went to the king and
reported to him.

The king was sad!
He felt bad!
Daniel was his friend.

But a rule is a rule,
and Daniel was arrested.

Big strong soldiers led
him to the lions' den.
R-R-R-ROAR!
The lions wanted to eat!

"May your God save you,"
the king said hopefully.

Whoosh! The soldiers threw Daniel
down, down, down.
There were HUNGRY
LIONS all around.

The king went home, but he could not eat.
He could not sleep.
He could not think about anything
but Daniel.

Early in the morning,
the king hurried out of bed
and scurried to see
if his friend was still alive.

"Did your God save YOU?"
he shouted anxiously.

Then he waited for an answer.

"YES!" Daniel called out.
"My God sent his angel
to shut the lions' mouths."

The king was so happy.
"Pull Daniel out of
the lions' den!" he commanded.

And then the king
made a NEW rule.
"From now on,
everyone in my kingdom
will pray to Daniel's
wonderful God!"

ME TOO!® B O O K S